How To Survive Corporate America 101

By Christopher Williams

How To Survive Corporate America 101

ISBN-13: 9798673150740

*Take what you love and
mix it with what you know,
then watch the magic happen.*

*Jesus, family, knowledge,
technology, art, music, & travel
are what I love.*

*Corporate America,
is what I know.*

Thank you for reading.

Table of Contents

Chapter 1

"Welcome to the Team"

Alright, so you got the job offer, the salary, and the benefits that you wanted (*well the ones you would accept, at least*). It's your first day on the job and you are dressed for success! You've just finished up your HR new hire orientation session and now it's time to meet your new team! This is actually a pretty big deal because the people you are about to meet will become a big part of your life for the next three to five years. If you think about it, you are going to spend at least forty hours a week working, eating, learning, and (*everyone's favorite*) meeting with this group of people. Every office setup is a little different. In some instances, your team will sit intermingled with other teams, whereas others you may have whole floors or halls where it's just your team.

In any case there are some very distinct personalities that EVERY team, department, or section has. You will definitely meet some of the personalities on this list, so pay attention and you can know what to expect from each of them. Now without further ado, in no particular order, good bad or indifferent, here is the co-worker personalities list:

1. The Jerk
2. The Shoveler

Let's kick things off with "The Jerk". This person will undoubtedly be one of the first people that you will meet. Since they are usually very forward, they won't have any problem spotting you as the new person and setting in for the attack. You can expect an immediate wisecrack about your outfit, hair, shoes, or anything really. The Jerk always wants to see if they can get a rise out of everyone, because they get a kick out of pissing everyone else off. Fortunately, you got this book first and you will learn a quick and easy way to diffuse The Jerk. The things to remember are to stay calm and say something that they won't expect to throw them off of their game. Here is an example exchange:

The Jerk: "Hey it's the new guy, nice tie!"

(In this example the office dress code usually doesn't wear ties, so they are attempting to make you feel out of place by calling extra attention to the fact that you are overdressed.)

You: "Well thanks! I wanted to make sure you would like it, so I stayed up all night making sure I picked the best one."

You can bet your ascot they won't see that one coming! Now you have simultaneously let them know that they picked the wrong person to mess with, while also showing your new co-workers that you can think quickly on your feet.

A good thing about The Jerk is that they will keep you on your toes and require you to consistently bring your "A" game. Just appreciate them for what they can do to improve you along the way, even if they are extremely annoying in the process. One last tip about The Jerk, they usually only mess with you if they like you so consider it their personal way of saying "Welcome to the Team!"

Our next very interesting personality is "The Shoveler". On the surface they can seem like very nice people, but in reality, they are hiding a dirty little secret; they hate to have any new types of work assigned to them.

You see, they often have an extremely limited skill set and the idea of doing any work outside of those limited skills terrifies them to the core. As a result of this fact, anytime any work comes their way that they are even slightly uncomfortable or unfamiliar with, they will shovel it onto someone else as quickly as possible with reckless abandon to get it off their plate. They will usually open up with something simple like "Hey can you have a look at this?" Then as soon as you take that look, in their eyes you now own that particular assignment and all future ones like it for all eternity.

Another sneaky trick they like is find any part of the task that even remotely relates to your area and then use that as a catalyst to ask you to have a look at it. One last tactic that The Shoveler will use is to attempt to appear extremely busy in an effort to avoid getting assigned any new work. They will take the most mundane task and make it sound like quantum physics so it gives the impression that they couldn't possibly have the time to take on anything else. They are masters at their craft and will always look for any and every excuse to get the work off them and onto someone else, so don't let it be you!

Now if you all would kindly indulge me for but a moment, I shall take this opportunity to introduce you to the illustrious stronghold of mental stability and scholarly acumen embodied in the technical astuteness of the person I have indubitably dubbed, "The Guru". I'll admit that introduction may have been a bit over the top, but you will soon find out why The Guru deserves every bit of pomp and circumstance for an introduction. Ironically, this person can usually be found in an unassuming office or cubicle in a back corner somewhere, mostly keeping to themselves.

They are typically very reserved and have already forgotten more than you will ever know. The Guru is called such because they can understand things on an entirely different level than most people. The Guru can take a task that you think is nearly impossible and crank it out like its nothing using the same tools that you have access to. They have a unique mix of raw talent and cultivated experience that gives them the decisive edge in anything that they set out to accomplish. They are often very approachable with a willingness to share their vast knowledge and talents.

You should always make it a point to identify and befriend the Guru early on because they will not only make your life a lot easier, they are generally just good people to be around which will in turn make you better. The Guru is also fully aware that they are such and can spot your fledgling efforts from a mile away. They will usually be the first ones to step in and save your bacon when you are in way over your head because they care about the next generation of workers coming up behind them and rarely ever miss an opportunity to rear someone up in the proper way to do something.

On any well-rounded team you will find our next individual who I like to affectionately call "The Old Timer". They are usually well into retirement age and have already actually retired from one or two previous careers but are now just working for the sheer joy of being useful and interacting with other people. Don't make the mistake of writing off The Old Timer as irrelevant or senile. More often than not, they will be so much older than you that they will have lived the equivalent of two to three of your lifetimes.

This gives them all kinds of insights on things and life experiences that you simply will not have had if you are a younger person. Make sure that you are <u>never</u> too busy to just sit and listen to any stories that The Old Timer is willing to share, even if they aren't work related at all. These legends of old are often packed with golden nuggets that can give you valuable advice on things that they wish they would have known when they were your age. The Old Timer can still be razor sharp on their skills, so if they interrupt you suddenly be quiet and listen to them even if you are teaching them something, because they might just surprise you and show you something that you didn't know.

Ok so what can we say can about this next personality? All offices have what I have found out to be "The Strange One" in the bunch. All types of things meet the minimum qualification standards for holding the title of the "The Strange One". They can range from overtly pervy, to poor hygiene, to unusual dress habits, to awkward social skills, etc. They typically aren't much of a threat to anyone, but they are just, well strange! Expect long rambling stories without ever reaching a valid point, constant oversharing of personal information to the point of disgust, pop culture references unknown to all but them, and lots of odd facial expressions and body posturing.

At the end of the day you have to be nice to everyone in the office, but my advice would be to keep a bit of distance between yourself and The Weird One. You never know when they might inadvertently cross a line with a company policy, or a powerful person and you certainly don't want to be dragged down along with them by association (*believe me I have seen it happen more than once*). In summary, never be mean to anyone, but keep it cordial and then keep it moving!

The last personality on our list that you might run into is "The Lazy One". They would basically end up being "The Shoveler" except for the fact that they are so lazy they won't even shovel off the work; they just simply don't do it. The crazy thing about The Lazy One is that they have such a reputation for being lazy that no one even wants to give them anything to do because they already know it will never get done.

The Lazy One has loads of free time since they don't actually do any work, and they usually spend the entire day up and down the hallway chatting about absolutely nothing or aimlessly surfing the internet in their office. It's really a marvel how they are able to keep a job for doing pretty much nothing at all but then again no one actually wants to deal with them, so the cycle just continues. I would write more about them, but I just don't feel like it (*see what I did there*).

The rest of your team will be regular ol' normal folks, so you can relax in knowing that some of the more challenging personalities will be few and far between. Now that you have met the team and know what you can expect from some of them, we can move on to our next chapter.

Chapter 2

"The Management Guild"

Unless you just got hired to be the new CEO (*yeah right*) you will not only have a manager, you will have an entire management chain of command! This is a nice way of saying instead of having one boss you could potentially have anywhere from five to seven bosses any of which could potentially give you something to do! Ok in reality any of them *could* give you something to do, but you will only realistically get work assigned to you by your direct manager and possibly his manager from time to time.

You will want to immediately know who's who in your organization and let me be the first to tell you looks can be deceiving. The person who looks like they wouldn't be in charge of anything might turn out to be the Executive Vice President of the entire Division. Meanwhile, the person who looks like they should be in charge of a whole lot of things could turn out to be just an individual contributor with no direct reports at all. If your company has an online photo directory, then find yourself in it and follow your management tree up until you get to the very top. Learn these faces and names so that you can have your best foot forward when they come around or if you end up on an email chain with one of their names.

Now let's talk about the different types of management styles that you may encounter. Just like with the team there are different personalities and styles of managers as well. From my experience there are four types of management styles that I see over and over again in Corporate America:

1. The Micro Manager
2. The Hands-Off Manager
3. The Cool Manager
4. The A-hole Manager

"The Micro Manager" is the prime minister of all things nitpicky and negligible with regard to your work and how you are doing it. Even though they are nice in personality they personify in complete totality the phrase, "you can't see the forest for the trees". They can spend an exhaustive amount of time dwelling on things like font size, word choice, and word order. Most people would never even notice the things that The Micro Manager is hyper focused on. They will constantly be looking over your shoulder to make sure you are dotting every "i" and crossing every "t".

Expect to have to give constant updates and reupdates about tasks to give them the reassurance that you actually know what you are doing. At times they may even make you completely redo assignments just so they are completed "their way" even if you ultimately end up at the same goal! Every time you are late or want to take vacation time, they will have lots of questions about why and what it is that you were doing or are going to do.

Most people just simply cannot deal with a manager that constantly second guesses and double checks every aspect of every single thing that they do all day every day. Most managers that fall into this category end up with only 1 or 2 direct reports or a large percentage of new hires that don't know any better, because more seasoned employees will run from them in pursuits of being treated like an actual adult.

Being simultaneously a blessing and a curse is the polar opposite of "The Micro Manager"; our beloved "Hands Off Manager". The best thing about The Hands Off Manager is also the worst thing about them; they are completely hands off with regard to you and your work. If you are a self-driven person then you will click extremely well with this management style. You may go days or weeks at a time without so much as speaking to or even seeing The Hands Off Manager! I can't tell if this management style leans more toward their extreme trust in your abilities or if they just simply do not care about what you are doing as long as no one is asking them about you. Heck for all I know it could be both, but regardless, you are on you own.

Now this can lead to issues if you find yourself struggling in an area of growth or with a particular assignment. Remember they are hands-off in their approach so just like they aren't constantly hovering over you when you are comfortable, don't expect for them to realize that you need help and swoop in to save you. Another challenge is you may not hear from them for two weeks, but then out of the blue they may want an update on everything you have going on, and right now. This requires you to manage your own affairs so that you can give all of the necessary updates that you are asked to and then they can go back to what they were doing. All things considered, as long as you are organized and can find other sources of help this can actually be a great management style to fall under.

This next style of management is the Holy Grail of styles to find yourself under. "The Cool Manager" is such a down to earth individual and they truly "get it" when you need to them to. Whether you need to take an hour to run to the DMV in the middle of the day, have a sick kid at daycare or school, or you just need to head out a few minutes early even though you were late you will always get a variant of "Hey as long as everything gets done its fine with me." The Cool Manager realizes that you are an adult and you know what you are responsible for at all times. They have high expectations for your work but trust you to get it done quickly and with the highest quality. This level of trust in you should cause you to respond with the utmost respect for them and your responsibilities.

Why would you want to take advantage of someone who isn't giving you a hard time and just expects you to do your job? You would be crazy to abuse this freedom and potentially loose it, so don't! Whenever they ask you to do something you will want to take care of it immediately because when you need them, they are going to be right there with you and for you. If you get stuck on an issue, they will be right next to you helping you to work through it even if it causes them to miss a meeting or their own work. They want you to succeed because when you win, they win too. This is the ultimate management style to be under because with The Cool Manager you don't work for them, you work <u>with</u> them!

Purposefully last and also least (*because they are chumps*) are nobody's favorite, "The A-hole Managers". Honestly, I really don't get this type of management style. They will go out of their way to be difficult and to make things difficult for you to accomplish anything. This style encompasses all of the negative characteristics of the first two styles of management and somehow still adds its own bit of chaos into the mix. Managers that graduated from this school of thought can sometimes be mean for seemingly no reason at all. They can even let your ethnicity, sexuality, body type, or even nationality become a contributing factor in their treatment toward you.

To make matters worse they also typically have a favorite employee that will get: special attention, select choice in the most premium of projects, the first promotions, and none of the bull malarkey that they give to you. Make no mistake you will not be able to win them over to like you. If you try to work your way onto their good side, you will only burn yourself out and all of your hard work will be ignored just for the favorite employee to do less than impressive things and receive praise on top of praise for them.

My advice if you find yourself under an A-hole Manager is to RUN! As soon as you are able to, find another position within the company away from them. If you cannot get out from under them and remain in the company, then leave the company altogether and get out of that toxic relationship before it has a chance to affect you negatively. Life is too short to be miserable under someone with authority over your means to provide for yourself financially. They will never appreciate you or respect you, so go find someone who will.

Chapter 3

"The Vernacular"

In every new environment there is a certain vernacular that can either shut you out or become your passport to delightful interactions with the people around you. The key is to learn the language of the people you are around so that you can communicate with them most effectively. For example, if you went to rural Japan but couldn't read or speak any Japanese you would have a very difficult time talking with most people or finding the things that you needed (*like the bathroom*). Your new office will be no different and is going to be filled with words, phrases, and sayings defined by the local culture that each office has. This chapter will introduce you to some of the Corporate American Vernacular (*CAV for short*) that I have learned along the way to give you a head start in your office dialogue capabilities! This is not an exhaustive list, but it should be enough to get you started:

"Let's level set here" – Let's get everyone to have a mutual understanding of this topic to avoid any further confusion.

"Long way around the barn" – Doing something in a way that is unnecessarily difficult when there is an easier way readily available.

"Beat a dead horse" – Continuing to discuss an already exhausted issue.

"CYA" or Cover your a** – Don't let yourself get into a situation where you are exposed by neglecting important details that could cause trouble for you or your team later on.

"Pie in the sky" – Describing something in an ideal situation.

"10,000 ft level" – Summarizing your details at a very high level leaving out the extremely technical pieces.

"Six in one, half a dozen in the other" – We are basically saying the same thing just in different ways.

"Low hanging fruit" – Tasks that can be completed with relative ease.

"Hooking and jamming" – Getting into a good grove of working.

"We can rock and roll now" – All of the roadblocks have been removed so now this task can finally be completed.

"Rockstar" – Someone who is extremely good at their job.

"Nonreturnable" – This task is coming from someone so high up that we have to do it, no matter what and with no questions asked.

"Coming down from on high" – This mandate is coming down from the highest levels of management so there is nothing that can be done to change it.

"It was a cluster" – A disorganized chaotic mess.

"Deliverables" – The promised items that are required to be delivered once a project is complete.

"Drinking from a firehose" – Trying to complete a set of tasks that are arriving in an extremely rapid fashion without stopping. Also trying to absorb large sets of new information very quickly, usually as a result of a new job.

"I'm drowning" – The amount work I have coming in has overwhelmed my ability to complete it all.

"I'm trying to keep my head above water" – I am trying to keep up with the steadily increasing work tasks that I am receiving.

"I'm trying to wrap my head around this" – The idea of this task is so daunting that I need more time to process how this is even going to work out in my mind.

"Milestones" – Key points in the project that signify progress is being made.

"I'm living the dream" – I really don't like coming here every day, but I have bills to pay so I'm stuck.

"Flavors" – A fun way to say versions.

"Let me drive for a second" – I would like to use your keyboard and mouse to show you this instead of trying to talk you through it.

These phrases or variants of them will be floating around the office in meetings, breakrooms, and down the hallways. Knowing what people are really saying when they use this vernacular will give you a leg up when you hear it in action!

Chapter 4

"The Meetings Crash Course"

It is next to impossible to work anywhere in Corporate America and not eventually find yourself in a meeting about one thing or another. Meetings are a way of life in the office world and you need to know how to navigate them if you want to be successful in your career. There are several different types of meetings that you will experience, and they include:

1. One-on-One
2. Staff or Department
3. Dial In

One-on-One meetings are a chance for your direct manager or supervisor to spend some time with you and find out how things are going with your project(s). This is a good time to talk about any challenges that you are having with anything or to celebrate successes that you have achieved. Sometimes you will have an office setup where your manager will not be intimately involved in everything that you do, so these meetings are a good time to make them aware of the awesome work that you have accomplished. Before you attend these meetings make sure you have all of your project updates cleanly organized so that you can readily access them when you need to.

Don't be afraid to also use this time to get to know your manager on a more personal level if the opportunity arises. Managers are people too and sometimes they would rather just talk about personal interests and hobbies than work. You might find out you have some things in common with them and that will give you a stronger bond with your manager as a person, which is always a good thing. A final point about the One-on-One meeting is that not all managers do this by default, so you can always ask to have this type of meeting setup between you and your manager if they don't already have it as a part of their normal cadence.

Usually, your team or department will have a regular meeting about once or twice a month where you all come together to discuss different things related to the team. Sometimes these meetings will have a "let's go around the room" aspect to them where everyone will give a high-level update about something that they are working on. These meetings usually aren't too bad, but if we are being honest no one really cares about hearing updates from other projects that have nothing to do with them. The main thing in these meetings is to just try to look alert and stay awake.

Make sure your phone is on silent when you attend these meetings, because it will be very embarrassing when it sounds off while also vibrating and then everyone turns and looks at you while you scramble to get it silenced. Be sure to slowly nod your head while people are talking from time to time, so it really seems like you are engaged and understanding what they are saying. Sometimes you can even bring your laptop and just keep working on your own work, but don't become so engaged that you aren't paying attention to the general discussion going on around you.

If I ignored the fact that I hate meetings altogether and had to pick a favorite, then it would definitely be the Dial In meeting. The reason I like this type of meeting is that you can participate from the comfort of your own office, cubicle, car, or bed! Dial In meetings actually come in several different flavors (*Vernacular!*). There are some calls where the only things you say the whole time are hello and goodbye. Sometimes people will invite you to dial in just because you are a part of a certain team.

They may end up not needing you specifically on the call but it's easier to just have you available in case they do. In other calls you may only have to give an update or just answer a few questions. Then there are the calls where you have to talk almost the entire time. Having several of these types of calls in a row can be very draining, so try to space them throughout the day if you know you will have to do the bulk of the speaking.

If we can stay on Dial In calls for just a bit more there are two skills that I need to teach you how to use wisely. The first skill is called the "Name Radar". You can only use this one on calls where you don't think you will have to say anything at all, or on calls where you only have to answer a few random questions here and there. The more you have to talk in a Dial In meeting, the riskier this skill is to use so be careful. The Name Radar is essentially training your brain to only pay attention to the words that sound like your name and completely ignore the words that don't.

This will allow you to tune out the call as mostly background noise but tune back in when you hear your name so you can start paying attention again. Now the risky part about this is you will completely miss any information before you hear your name, so if they just asked you a question you will have no idea what it was. The key here is to smoothly extract the information you missed without blatantly admitting that you weren't paying any sort of attention to the call before they said your name. All you have to say is "I'm sorry I was multi-tasking, could you repeat that last part, again?" This is a very corporate way of admitting you were not listening without flat out saying it.

Another one you can use if you miss your name once or twice is "Sorry I was trying to get off of mute, can you say the last piece of what you just asked?" This one works because everyone at some point has minimized the phone app or conferencing program and then can't bring it back up fast enough when they need to say something. The most important thing to note is that you can only use this once maybe twice a day before people catch on to the fact that you are never paying attention. Just keep it in your toolbox and only use it when you need to.

The second skill is a simple one: always double then triple check that you are muted if you are not actively talking. I cannot tell you how many times someone has made a complete fool out of themselves by forgetting to mute their phone and then having some embarrassing background noise or saying something that you would never want the meeting attendees to actually hear. There is NO way out of this one if you mess up, and in some cases, it could cost you your job if you said something terrible enough or in front of a customer.

As an added bonus tip, I'll also say make sure that you have actually disconnected from the call when it ends. Sometimes your dial in application will not automatically end the call when the meeting time expires, and each participant will then have to manually hang up to actually end the call. This also applies if you end up having to share your screen during the call to illustrate something complicated. Forgetting to stop sharing your screen can be embarrassing too when you didn't realize you were still sharing, and the call didn't end automatically so the three stragglers left on the call are now watching you check your bank account or browse through your social media. Just make sure you fully disconnect when the call is over. Please.

Chapter 5

"Handling Pressure and Stress"

Working in Corporate America can come with lots of unique challenges as you go about your day-to-day work. One such challenge is how to manage the mounting pressure that can build up over time with regard to workload, work complexity, deadlines, and expectations. We all want to be successful in our careers and outside of charm and charisma, quality work is the key to accomplishing that goal. Not many people get promoted by blowing a budget, losing a customer, and then delivering a broken product.

Consistently delivering high quality results is one of the keys to being able to climb that corporate ladder. One thing you may begin to notice is that the more successful you become, the more work you will start to receive. Managers are also under a lot of pressure to deliver quality results, so when they have to figure out who to trust to get something done in a hurry they make sure to find their "go-to" people.

You could very well end up supporting upwards of four to five projects at the same time, and even if you manage to keep things moving along pressure and its cousin stress will inevitably be waiting for you. In the workplace stress and pressure are intimately connected because the more pressure you feel to get something done, the more stress you will experience trying to get it done. When you are supporting more than one project or account it can often seem like each one thinks that all you have to do all day is support them and no one else. They will often request your time as if you do not have four other accounts that also require your attention. So how do you go about making five different groups of people feel like they are your only customer without leaving anyone out in the cold? Your answer to this question will decide just how much pressure induced stress you will have in your career.

In my humble opinion, the correct way to answer this question is with honesty, transparency, and organization. If you have five demanding projects, then you are not going to be able to hide that fact from each project lead for long so why even try? Be honest with your project leads about the demands from your other project leads. They won't need many details but, this allows them to set their own internal expectations of both the types of requests that they make as well as reasonable timeframes to expect the work to be completed when they ask. They may not understand why it took you two weeks to complete a task if they don't know you also have four other people asking for the same types of tasks. Just be honest with them and make sure they understand your unique position.

Transparency is also required so that expectations can be managed properly. There are times when one project will be absolutely on fire and it will take up over 80% of your available time. Obviously, that only leaves 20% left for everyone else and that will not be enough time to take care of them all. You may want to let the remaining four project leads know that you have to give more attention to project number three to get them calmed down and then you will be able to resume things as they were for everyone else.

Most people will be ok with regular updates even if they are to say you are too busy, so at least they are aware of what is going on (*for a little while at least*). The issues start to arise when they have no idea what is taking you so long because you did not tell them anything. You have to let people know when you can't get to them and why so they can react and plan accordingly. Doing this eases the pressure because why would they ask you for something to be completed when they know you are not working on them today? If you don't tell them anything, they will start emailing you constantly and then if you don't respond, they will start copying your supervisor as well.

Now that the supervisor has been dragged into the fray, they will have their own set of questions and they will start emailing you too because now people are bothering them about you. Imagine this multiplied by four, with emails, calls, and questions from all of these project leads with your manager being copied all the while! Now you have an incredibly stressful situation that creates an enormous amount of pressure to complete all of their tasks, that in reality could have been avoided with some well-placed transparency in your communications.

The last way to keep the pressure and stress down is to stay organized. There is nothing worse than being so busy that you completely forget about something important and as a result it doesn't get completed. Work requests can come from multiple sources including verbal conversations, emails, tickets, and instant messages. I recommend having a folder for each project on your work computer to save all of your related correspondences. Once you have things all separated out, you can then put together task lists for each project that contain all of the requests that each is asking for.

Using these lists, you can track what has been completed versus what still needs to be completed so that you can prioritize tasks yourself. Organizing things in this fashion lets you easily prepare to give updates to the project leads so that when they ask you can tell them what has been done, what is currently being worked on, and what still needs to be done. If you find a few things that can be done very quickly then do them all together in one session. If you see tasks that are going to take longer you can plan out larger blocks of time to work on them. Never plan to work on bigger, more time-consuming tasks on days where you have lots of meetings, because you will need large uninterrupted blocks of time to concentrate.

By planning your tasks in advance, you can schedule your work around your meetings and knock out the quicker tasks when you have more meetings and the longer tasks when you don't have as many. You can also block out time on your calendar for longer tasks so if people do want to meet, they will see that you are busy and can pick another time.

In summary you have to be in control of things to keep the stress down. By being honest, transparent, and organized you are in the driver's seat and can more effectively manage the pressure which will in turn keep the stress down and give you a better quality of life in your career.

Chapter 6

"Being Yourself"

Some people may wonder from time to time, "Can I actually be myself at work, or should I be the version of myself that I think everyone wants me to be?" My answer to this would be as long as an aspect of your personality is not contradictive to professionalism, you would be doing your coworkers a disservice by denying them the chance to get to know that side of you. Let's say for example that you absolutely hate wearing shoes and socks at home. I would recommend not showing that side of yourself at work because it would be considered very unprofessional to walk around your office building in your socks, or heaven forbid barefoot!

Now on the other hand let's say you are really into reading comic books and have a large collection at home. If you brought in a few issues and displayed them on your desk, then that would be just fine (*as long as they are not graphic in nature*). You might even spark up a conversation with some fellow comic book lovers and build new relationships. Keeping this part of you hidden would have been a mistake because there is nothing about liking comic books that makes you unprofessional (*especially in the technical field*).

The thing about most folks in Corporate America is that they are terrified for anyone to get to know the real them. Some people even talk and act differently in the office because they think it will make them more accepted into the office culture. I personally disagree with this approach because it is simply too exhausting to pretend to be someone else all day. With this in mind I will introduce the "tone it down" mindset. See everyone has an experience where they may have to "tone it down" a bit. As an example, say there is a very loud and boisterous person who loves a good hardy laugh.

Now if this same person walks into a library, they will naturally "tone it down" because this is an environment known to be quiet by default. Once inside the library, this person will begin to talk and laugh more quietly but at the core everything about them remains the same. You see they have "toned it down" but not completely "switched" who they are. This is a very important point to make because you should <u>never</u> be made to feel like you have to change who you are to make someone else feel comfortable. You need to be free to be your true self wherever you are, especially in the workplace because you have to spend so much time there.

Some of the most successful people that I have seen are that way because they are not afraid to be themselves in all situations. A certain mental freedom comes from not having to worry about who you have to be to find acceptance. Some of the fear around being yourself may be about "letting people in", but rest assured your personality and intimate details of your personal life are two separate things. I would strongly advise against sharing intimate details of your personal life with coworkers because the more people know about you, the more control they will have over you. Your personality however should not apply to that rule as it can be a key to open doors around you that might otherwise be locked.

Do not ever be afraid to be the full you even if you have to "tone it down" a bit from time to time. You are a beautifully and wonderfully made person with unique ideas, talents, and perspectives that need to be shared with everyone who comes into contact with you. People will always respect and appreciate you more for being yourself as opposed to pretending to be someone else.

Chapter 7

"Knowing When to Move On"

At some point you may decide that your current role or company is no longer a good fit for you, and you may want to make a change. Navigating this process properly could land you in a new position that gives you access to things you did not have before. On the contrary, it could also leave you worse off than you were and also wondering why you ever left in the first place.

There could be several reasons why you might consider leaving a position or company altogether including management, salary, training opportunities, promotions, or even working conditions. The reason really does not matter, what's important here is that something about this current career path is starting to bother you and it's not going away. I think that if you could ignore whatever the issues were and just deal with it, then you would already be doing that.

With this in mind, the first step in knowing it is time for you to go is that you realize you can no longer ignore how unhappy this job is making you. Up until now you really haven't done anything concrete yet in one direction or another. Your manager and co-workers do not know anything yet so it's just you and your thoughts at this point. The time has now come to put some action behind your thoughts and get the ball rolling to your new career destination.

Researching what you want to do next will be the second step in knowing it is time to move on. Your company will more than likely have an internal job postings board or web portal that you can access. You should check here first because it's easier to move within the same company as opposed to leaving altogether. An added benefit to the internal postings is that you can usually see who the hiring manager is for the position. This will allow you to figure out if you even want to work for this person or not before you apply, which is a luxury you may not have if you look outside of your current company.

Another thing to consider by staying internal is that you won't be starting completely over in terms of years with the company, accrued vacation time, and existing relationships that could help you along. In most companies the longer you are there the more vacation time you have access to, so losing this is definitely something to consider if you like to travel or just take time off from work. If you simply cannot find anything inside the company for yourself then it may be time to start looking outside for your next career path.

Eventually though you will find something else and when you do, just make sure to have an honest conversation with yourself about whether this is a good move or not. Sometimes you may be jumping into a situation that is different but presents its own set of new challenges that you didn't have to worry about before. For example, let's say you hate having to be a part of an off hours on-call rotation as a part of your current job. You find out that the new job does not even have an on-call component, but they travel out of state every 2 months for a week at a time. If you love to travel then this may be a great thing, but if you have a family (*especially one with multiple kids*) travel could spell disaster for your situation.

How would your spouse handle getting all of the kids dropped off and picked up when you are gone? I can promise you this will get old very quickly and will cause new problems that you did not have to consider before. This is why you have to carefully consider all of the options when you change career paths. Sometimes the thing that caused you to want to leave might become the lesser of two evils by comparison. Of course, there will be other times where the new job will be everything you ever wanted it to be and then by all means you should go and never look back!

The reality of the situation is that you do eventually need to find a place where you can settle down and grow into your career, but you may have to hop around a bit before you find that special place. No company or position will ever be 100% perfect all of the time so don't drive yourself crazy by embarking on a never-ending quest to find it because it simply does not exist. You just need to find a company that values you and a job within it that you can deal with most of the time so that you can provide for yourself or your family.

Chapter 8

"Passion Projects"

Every single company is nothing more than a collection of people that are working together for a common goal. Usually that goal is to create a product or provide a service to paying customers. Within that though, some companies manage to rise above their base goals and focus attention on the people doing the work to make them feel valued and also to improve their interactions with each other.

Companies that truly value their employees will listen to them when they are passionate about something that can add value to the company even if it is indirectly. Once such way to add value to your company is through what I like to call a "Passion Project". I define a Passion Project as work on top of the company's bottom line goals that seeks to improve either the image or environment of said company through the volunteer work of its employee(s) that share a common passion.

There really is no format to a Passion Project as they can be about anything a group of employees becomes excited about. As an example, let's say a company has a large population of employees over the age of 50 and they have recently started hiring a lot of younger employees. Chances are most events, perks, and culture of the company are currently catered to an over 50 crowd so the new younger people may start to feel left out or even ignored. A Passion Project to them may be to create an internal organization that focuses on a younger crowd so new events for networking, socializing, and even career advancement can be planned.

This has absolutely nothing at all to do with the base line goals of the company, but you can bet that the younger people will be happier in their new interactions with each other now that they have found a place to belong. As a result, their ideas will begin to flourish as they will have a more positive experience within the company. These ideas could become the new lifeblood of the company as they seek to stay relevant in an ever-changing economy.

Another example of a Passion Project could be that minority communities within the company are noticing that hiring is always done from the same universities and as a result the hiring pool is not very diverse. A Passion Project for them might be to work with the Human Resources department to diversify the recruiting efforts and then cultivate a collaborative minority culture within the company. As a result, the company is now building a more diverse employee base that brings all sorts of new and interesting perspectives that were not readily available before. The company will be much stronger as a result of this volunteer work to build diversity even though it had nothing to do with the company's bottom line goals.

Another benefit of embarking on a Passion Project is that when the benefits of your work start to become visible, the upper leadership in the company will almost certainly notice the added value that your work is providing. Having this kind of attention can be an invaluable asset that may give you all types of new opportunities that would have otherwise been unavailable to you. Passion Projects allow you to stand out from the crowd and become a shining star among your peers.

This is yet another reason to be your full self so that the company can reap all of the benefits from the awesome personality that you have to share with them. Just remember that the key ingredient for a successful Passion Project is a <u>true</u> excitement for whatever it is you are trying to pursue. If you try to do this just for personal gain you will be found out and it will not end well for you, so please only start one if you are in it for the right reasons.

Chapter 9

"Work/Life Balance"

No matter what your role is in a company you will eventually come to a point where you will have to start balancing the amount of time and energy you are putting into your job versus how much you are investing into your life outside of work. This is the fabled Work/Life Balance that you often hear about and yes, it is a real thing!

What can all too quickly be lost in our goings on is the fact that we work to live and not the other way around. The entire reason that most of us go to work is so that we can make enough money to have food and shelter (*and to pay those pesky bills*). Working to live is something humans have done for millennia to survive, but only recently have humans started living to work. It terrifies me to know that there are people out there who have become so dedicated to their careers that they would start to choose work and projects over family time.

This is going to hurt some of you, but you need to know that if you were to die today your office would be cleaned out within a week and within a month someone else would be sitting in your old office doing your old job. The company would not stop, there would be no interruption in business dealings, and things would move on like you were never there. Believe me I have seen this happen more than once. I have also literally seen people work their whole lives away and then actually die in the office. You need to understand, and I mean now, that life is too short to become so consumed by work that you miss the opportunity to live life to its fullest.

I'll tell you another story. Once I was working on a high-profile project and I wanted to take a few days off to see some family that was coming into town. I only get to see them about once a year if that, so I was really excited to get to spend some time with them. As it turns out there was going to be a customer call on the same Friday that I was going to be out. My account manager at the time could not believe that I was going to miss the meeting even though it was not critical for me to be there.

He actually tried to make me feel guilty for taking some time off and was convinced that I was making a mistake. Fortunately, I did not listen to him and took the time off anyway. We had an absolute blast playing games, eating, laughing, and just enjoying being around each other. To this day I still look back on that trip with fond memories. Well as it would turn out, within six months of that trip the customer ended up canceling their contract AND my account manager left the company for another job. Had I chosen work over family I would have missed out on one of the best trips ever just to attend a call for a customer who would be leaving anyway to please an account manager who isn't even there anymore.

Now don't get me wrong, there will be times where you have to go above and beyond in your job to accomplish specific goals and milestones, but they should be few and far between. If you find yourself constantly having to choose between work and family, then you are in the wrong career path and you need to find something else to do. If you have young children, then this doubly applies because they are only going to be young once and you will never get those precious moments back. No career is worth missing your child's first steps, first words, or other irreplaceable moments for.

Moving on to vacation time, you need to make sure that you use every single day of it each year that it is given to you. The only time that I can think of that you may want to save your vacation is if you are planning a trip that requires more time than you can accrue in a year. Carrying over large amounts of vacation days year after year with no real plans to use them is not an achievement or a badge of honor, rather it represents tons of missed opportunities to have had a great time enjoying life.

Never let a coworker make you feel bad for taking time off that the company gave to you. Some people are simply afraid to live and when they see you doing it, they become uncomfortable and will try to make you feel guilty about taking your vacation and living your best life. Forget about them, they can say whatever they want. I say book the trip, buy the plane tickets, and reserve the hotel!

Let's talk about some email etiquette to ensure that you can actually enjoy your vacation once you leave. There is nothing worse than being on vacation (*especially an expensive one*) only to get bombarded with constant phone calls and emails the whole time. A well-placed email before you go will be the key to making this work. It is customary to send out a note to your team and project leads detailing the dates of your time off and when you will be back to work.

If you don't mind a call or two while you are away, you should say "I will have limited access to email and phone while I am away". If you don't want any calls but will take them if you get one you should say "I will have extremely limited access to phone and email while I am away. Now if you want to go and be completely unbothered while you are gone you should say "I will have no access to phone or email while I am away". Remember you only have to tell them the dates of your trip not the details. For all they know you could be on a cruise ship in the middle of the ocean, or even deep in the mountains or woods.

Regardless of which option you choose, make sure you have your processes documented so that someone else can do them while you are away. You will also want to identify someone that can cover each of your areas of responsibility while you are gone. Something will <u>always</u> break as soon as you leave (*Murphy's Law*) so just cover your bases before the trip to ensure that you can have a great uninterrupted time!

You need to make sure that your work is done, but you have to live too. Please don't ever get so busy working that you forget how to live and just have fun. God gave us a big beautiful world to explore so go see as much of it as you can while you can! Trust me the work will still be there when you get back.

Oh, and if you can, bring a little something back for your team from wherever you went if you take a nice trip. Your coworkers *did* hold down the fort while you were away so this is a nice gesture to say thank you for making it so I could leave by handling my work while I was gone.

Chapter 10

"Lessons Learned"

Over the years I that have worked in Corporate America I have learned many lessons along the way, so I wanted to pass a few of them along to you. These are things that I thought would be good to know but that didn't necessarily fit into one of the previous chapters.

Lesson one is be careful who you piss off. The office world can sometimes place an opportunity in the lap of someone that you never expected them to have. This is not to say that they didn't deserve the opportunity, just that you did not expect them to receive it. One of the most prevalent examples that I have seen to illustrate this is with promotions to management positions. Someone could be literally be your co-worker today and in three years they might end up being your supervisor.

This has happened to me no less than three times in my own career. Now imagine if I had been a complete jerk to any of them when we were on the same level. How much of an idiot would I feel like to now have to report to someone that I used to be mean to. Furthermore, now that they have authority over me, I'm the one that is potentially in a position to receive mean treatment. I have also seen people receive mistreatment due to their gender or ethnicity only for that same person to rise through the ranks and end up having all of those same people reporting to them. It's better just to be nice to everyone because you never know who is getting that next promotion to management.

Lesson two is don't sell yourself short when you don't know something. I'll let you in on a little secret. Just because people act confident in meetings or on calls, does not mean that they know everything or have all of the answers. I have been on lots of calls where I had no clue what the right answer was, so I just admitted that. To my surprise no one on the call knew the answer either and that led to new conversations about what to do to find a resolution. Unless it is a basic core skill related to your job (*or something you really are supposed to know*) it's perfectly OK to admit that you don't know something. Sometimes others are just waiting for someone to break the ice and admit the truth because they are afraid to acknowledge it themselves.

Lesson three is never be afraid to speak up if you have an idea or if you know something is not going to work. I used to have a real fear of giving my opinion in meetings because I would always assume everyone in the meeting was so much smarter or knowledgeable than I was. One particular time I was on a call and I was chatting with a coworker over instant messenger who was also in the same call. We heard someone say something that I knew was a terrible idea and I also knew the exact reason why it was not going to work. Everyone on the call seemed oblivious to this fact and was ready to adopt the idea and move on. I remember messaging my coworker that this would never work because of reasons x, y, and z.

On some level I wanted my coworker to step up and tell them what I was thinking, but instead they responded (*in all caps if I remember correctly*) "WELL SPEAK UP!" In that moment I realized that there was no reason why I shouldn't say what I was thinking so I did, and we ended up avoiding a decision that would have led to a lot of wasted time and effort. You have ideas, magnificently great ideas that no one has heard yet. Speak up and let them be heard, because for all you know that idea could be the new direction that the project needed to survive!

Lesson four is to dive in headfirst when you don't know what you are doing. Sometimes you will get assigned a new project that you won't know where to even begin to get started. Diving in headfirst means, finding all of the documentation that you can, scheduling meetings with people who are familiar with the work you are doing, and just getting started anywhere. You will be surprised how much you can learn about something as long as you have a clear directive as to what it is you are supposed to accomplish. Google is your biggest weapon in your quest for knowledge. Someone out there has had this problem before so search diligently to find their experience and learn from it.

Sometimes it may not be your exact issue but it's close enough to help you figure out the solution to your problem. Sometimes the scariest part about getting started is actually just getting started. More often than not I have found that if I just start trying to figure it out, the initial fear is quelled by the act of just starting. Always try your best in everything that you do, after all how can you do any better than your very best right? Giving everything your best shot will usually be enough to land you on the side of success. You are more talented than you know, so just get started!

Our final lesson is this: always speak to the person not the position title that the person has. No matter who I come across from the custodian to the Chief Executive Officer (*and yes, I have actually met both in several situations in different companies*) I always treat everyone the same. Sure they may be the Senior Vice President of

Research and Development, but they are still a person. They get tired, hungry, angry, and nervous just like anyone else. So when I meet them I never speak to the Senior Vice President of Research and Development, I speak to Robert, or Stephanie, or whatever their name might be.

No one really wants to be treated like a commodity or an object and that's exactly what a title is. A title is not the person and the person is not their title. On the other end of the spectrum, if you treat a person with a high-ranking position better, do you treat a person with a lower ranking position worse? Do you treat the custodian or food service worker with less respect because of their title? I would implore you to always treat everyone the same no matter what their job may be.

These people are not "the help", they are people and deserve to be treated as such. Please just treat everyone you meet with the utmost dignity and respect that they are entitled to as fellow humans on this planet that we all share together. We are all the same and we are all different. We should always celebrate our similarities and never forget to honor our differences.

One last thing I want to say is thank you to each and every person that bought and read this book. You guys are the best and I really appreciate you taking a chance on something that I wrote. I wish all of you the very best in your respective careers and it is my sincere hope that the words in this book will help each of you in your work encounters to achieve the success that I know you all are capable of.

Take Care!